Supply Short Contract

This contract should be used for local and international procurement of goods under a single order or on a batch order basis and is for use with contracts which do not require sophisticated management techniques and impose only low risks on both the Purchaser and the Supplier

An NEC document

April 2013

Construction Clients' Board endorsement of NEC3

The Construction Clients' Board recommends that public sector organisations use the NEC3 contracts when procuring construction. Standardising use of this comprehensive suite of contracts should help to deliver efficiencies across the public sector and promote behaviours in line with the principles of *Achieving Excellence in Construction*.

Cabinet Office UK

NEC is a division of Thomas Telford Ltd, which is a wholly owned subsidiary of the Institution of Civil Engineers (ICE), the owner and developer of the NEC.

The NEC is a family of standard contracts, each of which has these characteristics:

- Its use stimulates good management of the relationship between the two parties to the contract and, hence, of the work included in the contract.

- It can be used in a wide variety of commercial situations, for a wide variety of types of work and in any location.

- It is a clear and simple document – using language and a structure which are straightforward and easily understood.

NEC3 Supply Short Contract is one of the NEC family and is consistent with all other NEC3 documents. Also available are the Supply Short Contract Guidance Notes and Flow Charts.

ISBN (complete box set) 978 0 7277 5867 5
ISBN (this document) 978 0 7277 5897 2
ISBN (Supply Short Contract Guidance Notes and Flow Charts)
978 0 7277 5935 1

First edition 2009
Reprinted 2010
Reprinted with amendments 2013

British Library Cataloguing in Publication Data for this publication is available from the British Library.

Typeset by Academic + Technical, Bristol

Printed and bound in Great Britain by Bell & Bain Limited, Glasgow, UK

FOREWORD

I was delighted to be asked to write the Foreword for the NEC3 Contracts.

I have followed the outstanding rise and success of NEC contracts for a number of years now, in particular during my tenure as the 146th President of the Institution of Civil Engineers, 2010/11.

In my position as UK Government's Chief Construction Adviser, I am working with Government and industry to ensure Britain's construction sector is equipped with the knowledge, skills and best practice it needs in its transition to a low carbon economy. I am promoting innovation in the sector, including in particular the use of Building Information Modelling (BIM) in public sector construction procurement; and the synergy and fit with the collaborative nature of NEC contracts is obvious. The Government's construction strategy is a very significant investment and NEC contracts will play an important role in setting high standards of contract preparation, management and the desirable behaviour of our industry.

In the UK, we are faced with having to deliver a 15–20 per cent reduction in the cost to the public sector of construction during the lifetime of this Parliament. Shifting mind-set, attitude and behaviour into best practice NEC processes will go a considerable way to achieving this.

Of course, NEC contracts are used successfully around the world in both public and private sector projects; this trend seems set to continue at an increasing pace. NEC contracts are, according to my good friend and NEC's creator Dr Martin Barnes CBE, about better management of projects. This is quite achievable and I encourage you to understand NEC contracts to the best you can and exploit the potential this offers us all.

Peter Hansford

UK Government's Chief Construction Adviser
Cabinet Office

PREFACE

The NEC contracts are the only suite of standard contracts designed to facilitate and encourage good management of the projects on which they are used. The experience of using NEC contracts around the world is that they really make a difference. Previously, standard contracts were written mainly as legal documents best left in the desk drawer until costly and delaying problems had occurred and there were lengthy arguments about who was to blame.

The language of NEC contracts is clear and simple, and the procedures set out are all designed to stimulate good management. Foresighted collaboration between all the contributors to the project is the aim. The contracts set out how the interfaces between all the organisations involved will be managed – from the client through the designers and main contractors to all the many subcontractors and suppliers.

Versions of the NEC contract are specific to the work of professional service providers such as project managers and designers, to main contractors, to subcontractors and to suppliers. The wide range of situations covered by the contracts means that they do not need to be altered to suit any particular situation.

The NEC contracts are the first to deal specifically and effectively with management of the inevitable risks and uncertainties which are encountered to some extent on all projects. Management of the expected is easy, effective management of the unexpected draws fully on the collaborative approach inherent in the NEC contracts.

Most people working on projects using the NEC contracts for the first time are hugely impressed by the difference between the confrontational characteristics of traditional contracts and the teamwork engendered by the NEC. The NEC does not include specific provisions for dispute avoidance. They are not necessary. Collaborative management itself is designed to avoid disputes and it really works.

It is common for the final account for the work on a project to be settled at the time when the work is finished. The traditional long period of expensive professional work after completion to settle final payments just is not needed.

The NEC contracts are truly a massive change for the better for the industries in which they are used.

Dr Martin Barnes CBE

Originator of the NEC contracts

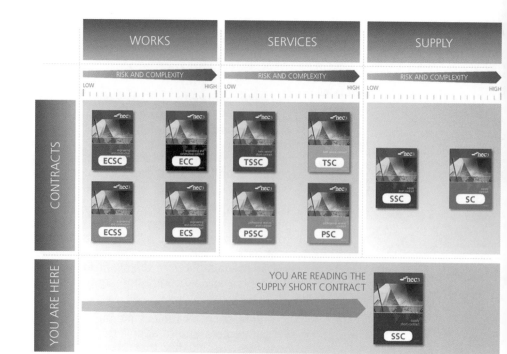

ACKNOWLEDGEMENTS

The first edition of the Supply Short Contract was produced by the Institution of Civil Engineers through its NEC Panel. It was mainly drafted by J. J. Lofty and P. A. Baird with the assistance of N. C. Shaw and J. M. Hawkins.

The Flow Charts were produced by Ross Hayes.

The original NEC was designed and drafted by Dr Martin Barnes then of Coopers and Lybrand with the assistance of Professor J. G. Perry then of the University of Birmingham, T. W. Weddell then of Travers Morgan Management, T. H. Nicholson, Consultant to the Institution of Civil Engineers, A. Norman then of the University of Manchester Institute of Science and Technology and P. A. Baird, then Corporate Contracts Consultant, Eskom, South Africa.

The members of the NEC Panel are:

N. C. Shaw, FCIPS, CEng, MIMechE (Chairman)
F. Alderson, BA (Melb), Solicitor
P. A. Baird, BSc, CEng, FICE, M(SA)ICE, MAPM
M. Codling, BSc, ICIOB, MAPM
L. T. Eames, BSc, FRICS, FCIOB
M. Garratt, BSc(Hons), MRICS, FCIArb
J. J. Lofty, MRICS

NEC Consultant:

R. A. Gerrard, BSc(Hons), FRICS, FCIArb, FCInstCES

Secretariat

J. M. Hawkins, BA(Hons), MSc
S. Hernandez, BSc, MSc

AMENDMENTS APRIL 2013

The following amendments have been made to the December 2009 edition. Full details of all amendments are available on www.neccontract.com.

Page	Clause	Line	
3			Last paragraph replace: 'December 2009' with 'April 2013'
CC 5	51.1	1	replace: 'The *Purchaser* pays' with 'Each payment is made'
CC 6	62.3	1	new clause
	62.3	1	'62.3' now '62.4'
CC 7	62.4	1	'62.4' now '62.5'
	63.6	3	insert: 'The cost of preparing quotations for compensation events is not included in the assessment of compensation events.'
	63.8	1	new clause
	63.8	1	'63.8' now '63.9'
CC 9	90.4	1	replace: 'made a payment' with 'paid an amount due under the contract'

Short Contract

A contract between ....

....

....

and ....

....

....

for ....

....

....

> Notes about this contract are printed in boxes like this one. They are not part of the contract. Further guidance is provided in the NEC3 Supply Short Contract Guidance Notes.

contract forms

conditions of contract

www.neccontract.com

Contract Data

The *Purchaser* is

Name ....

Address ....

Telephone ....

E-mail address ....

The *Purchaser* requires the *Supplier* to Provide the Goods when instructed by Batch Order   Yes/No (delete as appropriate)

The *goods* are ....

The *law of the contract* is ....

The *period for reply* is .... weeks.

The *starting date* is ....

The *delivery date* is ....

> **If the *goods* are instructed by Batch Order enter here 'The *delivery date* is identified in the Batch Order'.**

The *premises* are ....

The period for the correction of Defects after Delivery is .... weeks.

The *defects date* is .... weeks after Delivery.

The *delay damages* are .... per day.

> **If the *goods* are instructed by Batch Order enter a *delay damages* amount appropriate to the quantity or use of the *goods* in the Batch.**

The *assessment day* is the .... of each month.

If the *goods* are instructed by Batch Order

the *batch order interval* is ....

the *end date* is ....

the quantity range of *goods* in a batch is   from .... to ....

2

Contract Data

The *Adjudicator* is

Name ....

Address ....

Telephone ....

E-mail address ....

The interest rate on late payment is .... % per complete week of delay.

> Enter a rate only if a rate less than 0.5% per week of delay has been agreed.

The *Supplier*'s liability to the *Purchaser* for indirect or consequential loss, including loss of profit, revenue and goodwill is limited to ....

The *Supplier* is not liable to the *Purchaser* for loss of or damage to the *Purchaser*'s property in excess of .... for any one event.

The *Purchaser* provides this insurance

> Only enter details here if the *Purchaser* is to provide insurance.

....

....

The *Adjudicator nominating body* is ....

The *tribunal* is ....

If the *tribunal* is arbitration, the arbitration procedure is ....

The *conditions of contract* are the NEC3 Supply Short Contract April 2013 and the following additional conditions

> Only enter details here if additional conditions are required.

....

....

....

....

contract forms

conditions of contract

3

The *Supplier*'s Offer

The *Supplier* is

Name ....

Address ....

....

Telephone ....

E-mail address ....

The percentage for overheads and profit added to Defined Cost is .... %.

The *Supplier* offers to Provide the Goods in accordance with the *conditions of contract* for an amount to be determined in accordance with the *conditions of contract*.

The offered total of the Prices is   ....

Enter the total of the Prices from the Price Schedule.

Signed on behalf of the *Supplier*

Name ....

Position ....

Signature ....   Date ....

The *Purchaser*'s Acceptance

The *Purchaser* accepts the *Supplier*'s Offer to Provide the Goods

Signed on behalf of the *Purchaser*

Name ....

Position ....

Signature ....   Date ....

Price Schedule

Entries in the first four columns of this Price Schedule are made either by the *Purchaser* or the tenderer. If the *Supplier* is to be paid an amount for the item which is not adjusted if the quantity of goods in the item changes, the tenderer enters the amount in the Price column only, the Unit, Quantity and Rate columns being left blank.

If the *Supplier* is to be paid an amount for the item of goods which is the rate for the goods multiplied by the quantity supplied, the tenderer enters a rate for each item and multiplies it by the Quantity to produce the Price, to be entered in the final column.

Item number	Description	Unit	Quantity	Rate	Price
. . . .	. . . .	. . . .	. . . .	. . . .	. . . .
. . . .	. . . .	. . . .	. . . .	. . . .	. . . .
. . . .	. . . .	. . . .	. . . .	. . . .	. . . .
. . . .	. . . .	. . . .	. . . .	. . . .	. . . .
. . . .	. . . .	. . . .	. . . .	. . . .	. . . .
. . . .	. . . .	. . . .	. . . .	. . . .	. . . .
. . . .	. . . .	. . . .	. . . .	. . . .	. . . .
. . . .	. . . .	. . . .	. . . .	. . . .	. . . .
. . . .	. . . .	. . . .	. . . .	. . . .	. . . .
. . . .	. . . .	. . . .	. . . .	. . . .	. . . .
. . . .	. . . .	. . . .	. . . .	. . . .	. . . .
. . . .	. . . .	. . . .	. . . .	. . . .	. . . .
. . . .	. . . .	. . . .	. . . .	. . . .	. . . .
. . . .	. . . .	. . . .	. . . .	. . . .	. . . .
. . . .	. . . .	. . . .	. . . .	. . . .	. . . .
. . . .	. . . .	. . . .	. . . .	. . . .	. . . .
. . . .	. . . .	. . . .	. . . .	. . . .	. . . .

The total of the Prices

Goods Information

The Goods Information should be a complete and precise statement of the *Purchaser*'s requirements. If it is incomplete or imprecise there is a risk that the *Supplier* will interpret it differently from the *Purchaser*'s intention. Information describing the *Purchaser*'s requirements for the supply of the *goods*, including the information to be provided by the *Supplier* in connection with the supply of the *goods*, should be stated in the section headed Supply requirements.

1 Description of the *goods*

Give a detailed description of what *goods* the *Supplier* is required to supply. This may include drawings. Give the information of the required quality standards, the tests and inspections required and any health and safety requirements.

. . . .

. . . .

. . . .

. . . .

. . . .

. . . .

. . . .

2 Specifications

List the specifications that apply to this contract.

Title	Date or revision	Tick if publicly available
. . . .	. . . .	. . . .
. . . .	. . . .	. . . .
. . . .	. . . .	. . . .
. . . .	. . . .	. . . .
. . . .	. . . .	. . . .
. . . .	. . . .	. . . .
. . . .	. . . .	. . . .

Goods Information

3 Constraints on how the *Supplier* Provides the Goods

> State any constraints on how the *Supplier* is to provide the *goods* such as, any limits on subcontracting.

....

....

....

....

....

....

....

....

....

4 Requirements for the programme

> State whether a programme is required and, if it is, state what form it is to be in, what information is to be shown on it, when it is to be submitted and when it is to be updated.

....

....

....

....

....

....

....

....

....

www.neccontract.com

Goods Information

5 Services and other things provided by the *Purchaser*

> Describe what the *Purchaser* will provide, in connection with the supply of the *goods*, such as transport, loading or unloading of the *goods*.

Item	Date by which it will be provided
. . . .	. . . .
. . . .	. . . .
. . . .	. . . .
. . . .	. . . .
. . . .	. . . .
. . . .	. . . .
. . . .	. . . .

6 Supply requirements

> State the information which describes the *Purchaser*'s requirements (other than services he is to provide) in connection with the supply of the *goods* including the requirements for transport, the mode of transport and the loading and unloading of the *goods*.
>
> State the delivery place, the hours of access to the delivery place and other information to be provided by the *Supplier* at the time of Delivery such as the delivery note, which notifies the actual delivery date. The information necessary for a purchase that involves international, cross border transactions should be stated here, such as export and import requirements of the Customs authorities.

. . . .

. . . .

. . . .

. . . .

. . . .

. . . .

. . . .

contract forms

conditions of contract

nec®3 Supply Short Contract

CONDITIONS OF CONTRACT

1 General

Actions **10**

    10.1   The *Purchaser* and the *Supplier* shall act as stated in this contract and in a spirit of mutual trust and co-operation.

Identified and **11**
defined terms

    11.1   In the *conditions of contract*, terms identified in the Contract Data are in italics and defined terms have capital initials.

    11.2   (1) A Defect is a part of the *goods* which is not in accordance with the Goods Information.

(2) Defined Cost is an amount paid by the *Supplier* in Providing the Goods (excluding any tax which the *Supplier* can recover) for

- people,
- equipment,
- plant and materials to be included in the *goods* and
- transport

whether work is subcontracted or not.

(3) Delivery is when the *Supplier* has

- done all the work which the Goods Information states he is to do by the Delivery Date and
- corrected Defects which would have prevented the *Purchaser* from using the item of *goods* or others from doing their work.

(4) The Delivery Date is the *delivery date* unless later changed in accordance with this contract.

(5) Goods Information is information which

- specifies and describes the *goods* and
- states any constraints on how the *Supplier* Provides the Goods

and is in

- the document called 'Goods Information' or
- an instruction given in accordance with this contract.

(6) The Parties are the *Purchaser* and the *Supplier*.

(7) The Prices are the amounts stated in the price column of the Price Schedule. Where a quantity is stated for an item in the Price Schedule, the Price is calculated by multiplying the quantity by the rate.

(8) To Provide the Goods means to do the work necessary to supply the *goods* in accordance with this contract and all incidental work, services and actions which this contract requires.

contract forms

conditions of contract

Interpretation and the law	**12**	
	12.1	In this contract, except where the context shows otherwise, words in the singular also mean in the plural and the other way round and words in the masculine also mean the feminine and neuter.
	12.2	This contract is governed by the *law of the contract*.
	12.3	No change to this contract, unless provided for by the *conditions of contract*, has effect unless it has been agreed, confirmed in writing and signed by the Parties.
	12.4	This contract is the entire agreement between the Parties.
Communications	**13**	
	13.1	Each communication which this contract requires has effect when it is received in writing at the last address notified by the recipient for receiving communications.
	13.2	If this contract requires the *Purchaser* or the *Supplier* to reply to a communication, unless otherwise stated in this contract, he replies within the *period for reply*.
The *Purchaser*'s authority and delegation	**14**	
	14.1	The *Purchaser* may give an instruction to the *Supplier* which changes the Goods Information.
	14.2	After consultation with the *Supplier*, the *Purchaser* may instruct a change to the Delivery Date.
	14.3	The *Purchaser*'s acceptance of a communication from the *Supplier* or of his work does not change the *Supplier*'s responsibility to Provide the Goods.
	14.4	The *Purchaser*, after notifying the *Supplier*, may delegate any of the *Purchaser*'s actions and may cancel any delegation. A reference to an action of the *Purchaser* in this contract includes an action by his delegate.
Access and the provision of services	**15**	
	15.1	The *Purchaser* allows access to and use of the *premises* to the *Supplier* as necessary for the work included in this contract.
	15.2	The *Purchaser* provides services and other things as stated in the Goods Information.
Early warning	**16**	
	16.1	The *Supplier* and the *Purchaser* give an early warning by notifying the other as soon as either becomes aware of any matter which could

- increase the total of the Prices,
- interfere with the timing of the supply or
- impair the performance of the *goods* in use.

The *Supplier* may give an early warning by notifying the *Purchaser* of any other matter which could increase his total cost. Early warning of a matter for which a compensation event has previously been notified is not required.

	16.2	The *Supplier* and the *Purchaser* co-operate in making and considering proposals for how the effect of each matter which has been notified as an early warning can be avoided or reduced and deciding and recording actions to be taken.

(left margin tabs: contract forms / conditions of contract)

2 The *Supplier*'s main responsibilities

Providing the Goods **20**

20.1   The *Supplier* Provides the Goods in accordance with the Goods Information.

Subcontracting **21**

21.1   If the *Supplier* subcontracts work, he is responsible for Providing the Goods as if he had not subcontracted.

21.2   This contract applies as if a subcontractor's employees and equipment were the *Supplier*'s.

Other responsibilities **22**

22.1   The *Supplier* provides access for the *Purchaser* and others notified by the *Purchaser* to work being done and *goods* being stored for this contract.

22.2   The *Supplier* obeys an instruction which is in accordance with this contract and is given to him by the *Purchaser*.

22.3   The *Supplier* obtains permission from others where necessary before transporting the *goods* to the delivery place stated in the Goods Information.

22.4   The *Supplier* acts in accordance with the health and safety requirements stated in the Goods Information.

Batch Orders **23**

23.1   If the Contract Data states that the *Purchaser* requires the *Supplier* to Provide the Goods when instructed by Batch Order the following provisions apply

- A Batch Order is the *Purchaser*'s instruction to supply items of *goods* in a batch within a stated period of time.
- A Batch Order includes
  - a description of the *goods* in the batch,
  - the quantity of *goods* in the batch,
  - the start date and *delivery date* for the batch and
  - the prices for the items of *goods* in the batch and the total price of the batch.
- The *Purchaser* consults the *Supplier* about the contents of a Batch Order before he issues it.
- The period between the issue dates of each Batch Order is not less than the *batch order interval* stated in the Contract Data. The *Purchaser* extends or reduces the period if both Parties agree.
- The prices for items of *goods* in the batch are taken from the Price Schedule.
- The *Supplier* starts work on the batch when the *Purchaser* has issued the Batch Order.
- A Batch Order is not issued after the *end date*.
- The following are compensation events.
  - An item of *goods* required by the Batch Order is not included in the Price Schedule.
  - The total quantity of *goods* in the Batch Orders issued under this contract is different from that stated in the Price Schedule.
  - The quantity of *goods* stated in a Batch Order is not within the range stated in the Contract Data.

contract forms

conditions of contract

3 Time

Starting and Delivery	**30**	
	30.1	The *Supplier* does not start work until the *starting date* and does the work so that Delivery is on or before the Delivery Date.
Instructions to stop or not to start work	**31**	
	31.1	The *Purchaser* may instruct the *Supplier* to stop or not to start any work and may later instruct him to re-start or start it.
The programme	**32**	
	32.1	The *Supplier* submits programmes to the *Purchaser* for acceptance as stated in the Goods Information.

4 Testing and Defects

Tests and inspections	**40**	
	40.1	The *Purchaser* and the *Supplier* carry out tests and inspections required by the Goods Information. If a test or inspection shows that any *goods* have a Defect, the *Supplier* corrects the Defect and the test or inspection is repeated.
Notifying Defects	**41**	
	41.1	The *Purchaser* may notify a Defect at any time before the *defects date*.
Correcting Defects	**42**	
	42.1	The *Supplier* corrects a Defect whether or not the *Purchaser* notifies him of it.
	42.2	After Delivery, the *Supplier* corrects a notified Defect before the end of the period stated in the Contract Data. This period begins when the *Purchaser* has arranged the access necessary for the *Supplier* to correct the Defect.
Accepting Defects	**43**	
	43.1	The *Supplier* and the *Purchaser* may each propose to the other that the Goods Information should be changed so that a Defect does not have to be corrected.
	43.2	If the *Supplier* and the *Purchaser* are prepared to consider the change, the *Supplier* submits a quotation for reduced Prices or an earlier Delivery Date or both to the *Purchaser* for acceptance. If the *Purchaser* accepts the quotation, he gives an instruction to change the Goods Information, the Prices and the Delivery Date accordingly.
Uncorrected Defects	**44**	
	44.1	If the *Supplier* has not corrected a notified Defect within the time required by this contract, the *Purchaser* assesses the cost of having the Defect corrected by others and the *Supplier* pays this amount.

contract forms

conditions of contract

5 Payment

Assessing the amount due **50**

50.1   The *Supplier* assesses the amount due and, by each *assessment day*, applies to the *Purchaser* for payment. There is an *assessment day* in each month from the *starting date* until the month after the *defects date*.

50.2   The *Supplier*'s application for payment includes details of how the amount due has been assessed. The first application for payment is for the amount due. Other applications are for the change in the amount due since the previous payment.

50.3   The amount due is

- the Price for each lump sum item in the Price Schedule which the *Supplier* has completed,
- where a quantity is stated for an item in the Price Schedule, an amount calculated by multiplying the quantity which the *Supplier* has completed by the rate,
- plus other amounts to be paid to the *Supplier*,
- less amounts to be paid by or retained from the *Supplier*.

Any tax which the law requires the *Purchaser* to pay to the *Supplier* is included in the amount due.

50.4   The *Purchaser* corrects any wrongly assessed amount due and notifies the *Supplier* of the correction before paying the *Supplier*.

50.5   The *Supplier* pays *delay damages* at the rate stated in the Contract Data from the Delivery Date for each day until Delivery.

Payment **51**

51.1   Each payment is made within three weeks after the next *assessment day* which follows receipt of an application for payment by the *Supplier*.

51.2   Interest is paid if a payment is late or includes a correction of an earlier payment. Interest is assessed from the date by which the correct payment should have been made until the date when it is paid. Interest is calculated at the rate stated in the Contract Data or, if none is stated, at 0.5% of the delayed amount per complete week of delay.

6 Compensation events

Compensation events **60**

60.1   The following are compensation events.

(1) The *Purchaser* gives an instruction changing the Goods Information unless the change is in order to make a Defect acceptable.

(2) The *Purchaser* gives an instruction changing the Delivery Date.

(3) The *Purchaser* does not allow access to and use of the *premises* as necessary for the work included in this contract.

(4) The *Purchaser* does not provide services and other things which he is to provide as stated in this contract.

(5) The *Purchaser* gives an instruction to stop or not to start any work.

(6) The *Purchaser* does not reply to a communication from the *Supplier* within the period required by this contract.

contract forms

conditions of contract

(7) The *Purchaser* changes a decision which he has previously communicated to the *Supplier*.

(8) An event which is a *Purchaser*'s risk stated in this contract.

Notifying compensation events **61**

61.1 The *Supplier* notifies the *Purchaser* of an event which has happened or which he expects to happen as a compensation event if

- the *Supplier* believes that the event is a compensation event and
- the *Purchaser* has not notified the event to the *Supplier*.

If the *Supplier* does not notify a compensation event within four weeks of becoming aware of the event, he is not entitled to a change in the Prices or the Delivery Date unless the event arises from an instruction of the *Purchaser*.

61.2 If the *Purchaser* decides that an event notified by the *Supplier*

- arises from the fault of the *Supplier*,
- has not happened and is not expected to happen,
- has no effect upon the Defined Cost or upon Delivery or
- is not one of the compensation events stated in this contract

he notifies the *Supplier* of his decision that the Prices and the Delivery Date are not to be changed.

If the *Purchaser* decides otherwise, he instructs the *Supplier* to submit a quotation for the event. The *Purchaser* notifies the decision to the *Supplier* or instructs the *Supplier* to submit a quotation within one week of the *Supplier*'s notification to the *Purchaser* of the event.

61.3 If the *Purchaser* decides that the *Supplier* did not give an early warning of the event which the *Supplier* could have given, the *Purchaser* notifies that decision to the *Supplier* when instructing the *Supplier* to submit a quotation.

61.4 A compensation event is not notified after the *defects date*.

Quotations for compensation events **62**

62.1 A quotation for a compensation event comprises proposed changes to the Prices or rates and any delay to the Delivery Date assessed by the *Supplier*. The *Supplier* submits details of his assessment with each quotation. The *Supplier* submits a quotation within two weeks of being instructed to do so by the *Purchaser* or, if no such instruction is received, within three weeks of the notification of a compensation event.

62.2 The *Purchaser* may instruct the *Supplier* to submit a quotation for a proposed instruction or a proposed changed decision. The *Supplier* does not put a proposed instruction or a proposed changed decision into effect.

62.3 If the *Supplier* does not provide a quotation for a compensation event within the time allowed, the *Purchaser* assesses the compensation event and notifies the *Supplier* of his assessment.

62.4 The *Purchaser* replies within two weeks of the *Supplier*'s submission.

For a proposed instruction or proposed changed decision, the *Purchaser*'s reply is

- notification that the proposed instruction will not be given or the proposed changed decision will not be made,
- notification of the instruction or changed decision as a compensation event and acceptance of the quotation or
- notification of the instruction or changed decision as a compensation event and notification that the *Purchaser* does not agree with the quotation.

For other compensation events, the *Purchaser*'s reply is

- acceptance of the quotation or
- notification that the *Purchaser* does not agree with the quotation.

62.5   If the *Purchaser* does not agree with the quotation, the *Supplier* may submit a revised quotation within two weeks of the *Purchaser*'s reply. If the *Purchaser* does not agree with the revised quotation or if none is received, the *Purchaser* assesses the compensation event and notifies the *Supplier* of his assessment.

Assessing   63
compensation events   63.1   If the *Purchaser* and the *Supplier* agree, for a compensation event which only affects the quantities of *goods* shown in the Price Schedule, the change to the Prices is assessed by multiplying the changed quantities of *goods* by the appropriate rates in the Price Schedule.

63.2   For other compensation events, the changes to the Prices are assessed by forecasting the effect of a compensation event upon the Defined Cost or, if the compensation event has already occurred, the assessment is based upon the Defined Cost due to the event which the *Supplier* has incurred. Effects on Defined Cost are assessed separately for

- people,
- equipment,
- plant and materials included in the *goods*,
- work subcontracted by the *Supplier* and
- transport.

The *Supplier* shows how each of these effects is built up in each quotation for a compensation event. The percentage for overheads and profit stated in the *Supplier*'s Offer are applied to the assessed effect of the event on the Defined Cost except that it is not applied to any tax charges for customs clearance and export or import.

63.3   The effects of compensation events upon the Defined Cost are assessed at open market or competitively tendered prices with deductions for all discounts, rebates and taxes which can be recovered. The following are deducted from the Defined Cost for the assessment of compensation events

- the cost of events for which this contract requires the *Supplier* to insure and
- other costs paid to the *Supplier* by insurers.

63.4   A delay to the Delivery Date is assessed as the length of time that, due to the compensation event, Delivery is forecast to be delayed.

63.5   If the *Purchaser* has decided and notified the *Supplier* that the *Supplier* did not give an early warning of a compensation event which an experienced supplier could have given, the event is assessed as if the *Supplier* had given early warning.

63.6   Assessment of the effect of a compensation event includes risk allowances for cost and time for matters which are at the *Supplier*'s risk under this contract. The cost of preparing quotations for compensation events is not included in the assessment of compensation events.

63.7   Assessments are based on the assumptions that the *Supplier* reacts competently and promptly to the compensation event and that any additional cost and time due to the event are reasonably incurred.

63.8   Assessments for changed Prices for compensation events are in the form of changes to the Price Schedule.

63.9   The assessment of a compensation event is not revised if a forecast upon which it is based is shown by later recorded information to have been wrong.

contract forms

conditions of contract

7 Title

The *Purchaser*'s title to the *goods* **70**

70.1 Whatever title the *Supplier* has to the *goods* before they are brought within the delivery place stated in the Goods Information passes to the *Purchaser* if the *Supplier* has marked them as for this contract.

70.2 Whatever title the *Supplier* has to the *goods* passes to the *Purchaser* if they have been brought within the delivery place stated in the Goods Information.

Marking *goods* before Delivery **71**

71.1 The *Supplier* marks the *goods* before they are brought within the delivery place stated in the Goods Information if

- this contract identifies them for payment and
- the *Supplier* has prepared them for marking as the Goods Information requires.

8 Risks, indemnities, insurance and liability

Purchaser's risks **80**

80.1 The following are *Purchaser*'s risks.

- Claims, proceedings, compensation and costs payable which are due to
  - the unavoidable result of the supply of the *goods*,
  - negligence, breach of statutory duty or interference with any legal right by the *Purchaser* or by any person employed by or contracted to him except the *Supplier* or
  - a fault of the *Purchaser*.
- Loss of or wear or damage to the *goods* after Delivery except loss, wear or damage occurring before the *defects date* which is due to
  - a Defect which existed at Delivery,
  - an event occurring before Delivery which is not a *Purchaser*'s risk or
  - the activities of the *Supplier* after Delivery.
- Loss of or wear or damage to the *goods* retained by the *Purchaser* after Delivery after a termination, except loss, wear or damage due to the activities of the *Supplier* after Delivery following the termination.

The *Supplier*'s risks **81**

81.1 From the *starting date* until the *defects date* the risks which are not carried by the *Purchaser* are carried by the *Supplier*.

Loss of and damage to the *goods* **82**

82.1 Until the *defects date* and unless otherwise instructed by the *Purchaser*, the *Supplier* promptly replaces loss of and repairs damage to the *goods*.

Indemnity **83**

83.1 Each Party indemnifies the other against claims, proceedings, compensation and costs due to an event which is at his risk.

83.2 The liability of each Party to indemnify the other is reduced to the extent that events which are the other Party's risk contributed to the losses, claims, proceedings, compensation and costs. The reduction is in proportion to the extent that events which were at the other Party's risk contributed, taking into account each Party's responsibilities under this contract.

Insurance cover **84**

84.1 The *Supplier* provides insurance against loss of or damage to the *goods*, plant and materials from the *starting date* until Delivery and against any risks he carries under this contract between Delivery and the *defects date*. The *Supplier* does not provide an insurance which the *Purchaser* is to provide as stated in the Contract Data.

Insurance policies **85**

85.1 When requested by a Party the other Party provides certificates from his insurer or broker stating that the insurances required by this contract are in force.

Limitation of liability **86**

86.1 The *Supplier*'s liability to the *Purchaser* for the *Purchaser*'s indirect or consequential loss, including loss of profit, revenue or goodwill is limited to the amount stated in the Contract Data.

86.2 For any one event, the liability of the *Supplier* to the *Purchaser* for loss of or damage to the *Purchaser*'s property is limited to the amount stated in the Contract Data.

86.3 The limitation of liability applies in contract, tort or delict and otherwise to the extent allowed under the *law of the contract*.

9 Termination and dispute resolution

Termination and reasons for termination **90**

90.1 If either Party wishes to terminate the *Supplier*'s obligation to Provide the Goods, he notifies the other Party giving details of his reason for terminating. The *Purchaser* issues a termination certificate promptly if the reason complies with this contract. After a termination certificate has been issued, the *Supplier* does no further work necessary to Provide the Goods.

90.2 Either Party may terminate if the other Party has become insolvent or its equivalent (Reason 1).

90.3 The *Purchaser* may terminate if he has notified the *Supplier* that the *Supplier* has defaulted in one of the following ways and has not stopped defaulting within two weeks of the notification.

- Substantially failed to comply with this contract (Reason 2).
- Substantially hindered the *Purchaser* (Reason 3).
- Substantially broken a health or safety regulation (Reason 4).

The *Purchaser* may terminate for any other reason (Reason 5).

90.4 The *Supplier* may terminate if

- the *Purchaser* has not paid an amount due under the contract within ten weeks of the *assessment day* which followed receipt of the *Supplier*'s application for payment (Reason 6) or
- the *Purchaser* has instructed the *Supplier* to stop or not to start any substantial work or all work for a reason which is not the *Supplier*'s fault and an instruction allowing the work to re-start or start has not been given within eight weeks (Reason 7).

90.5 The *Purchaser* may terminate if an event which the Parties could not reasonably prevent has substantially affected the *Supplier*'s work for a continuous period of more than thirteen weeks (Reason 8).

Procedures on termination	**91**	
	91.1	On termination, the *Purchaser* may obtain the remaining *goods* from other suppliers.
	91.2	On termination, the *Supplier* returns to the *Purchaser* equipment and surplus things provided by the *Purchaser*.

Payment on termination **92**

92.1 The amount due on termination includes

- an amount due assessed as for normal payments and
- the cost of plant and materials ordered by the *Supplier* specifically for the *goods* which cannot be resold or used elsewhere and of which the *Supplier* has to accept delivery.

92.2 If the *Purchaser* terminates for Reason 1, 2, 3 or 4, the amount due on termination also includes a deduction of the forecast additional cost to the *Purchaser* of Providing the Goods.

Dispute resolution **93**

93.1 A dispute arising under or in connection with this contract is referred to and decided by the *Adjudicator*.

The *Adjudicator* 93.2 (1) The Parties appoint the *Adjudicator* under the NEC Adjudicator's Contract current at the *starting date*. The *Adjudicator* acts impartially and decides the dispute as an independent adjudicator and not as an arbitrator.

(2) If the *Adjudicator* is not identified in the Contract Data or if the *Adjudicator* resigns or is unable to act, the Parties choose a new adjudicator jointly. If the Parties have not chosen an adjudicator, either Party may ask the *Adjudicator nominating body* to choose one. The *Adjudicator nominating body* chooses an adjudicator within four days of the request. The chosen adjudicator becomes the *Adjudicator*.

(3) The *Adjudicator*, his employees and agents are not liable to the Parties for any action or failure to take action in an adjudication unless the action or failure to take action was in bad faith.

The adjudication 93.3 (1) A Party may refer a dispute to the *Adjudicator* if

- the Party notified the other Party of the dispute within four weeks of becoming aware of it and
- between two and four further weeks have passed since the notification.

If a disputed matter is not notified and referred within the times set out in this contract, neither Party may subsequently refer it to the *Adjudicator* or the *tribunal*.

(2) The Party referring the dispute to the *Adjudicator* includes with his referral information to be considered by the *Adjudicator*. Any more information is provided within two weeks of the referral. This period may be extended if the *Adjudicator* and the Parties agree.

(3) The *Adjudicator* may take the initiative in ascertaining the facts and the law related to the dispute. He may instruct a Party to take any other action which he considers necessary to reach his decision and to do so within a stated time.

(4) A communication between a Party and the *Adjudicator* is communicated to the other Party at the same time.

(5) If the *Adjudicator*'s decision includes assessment of additional cost or delay caused to the *Supplier*, he makes his assessment in the same way as a compensation event is assessed.

(6) The *Adjudicator* decides the dispute and notifies the Parties of his decision and his reasons within four weeks of the referral. This period may be extended by up to two weeks with the consent of the referring Party, or by any period agreed by the Parties.

If the *Adjudicator* does not notify his decision within the time allowed, either Party may act as if the *Adjudicator* has resigned.

(7) Unless and until the *Adjudicator* has notified the Parties of his decision, the Parties proceed as if the matter disputed was not disputed.

(8) The *Adjudicator*'s decision is binding on the Parties unless and until revised by the *tribunal* and is enforceable as a matter of contractual obligation between the Parties and not as an arbitral award. The *Adjudicator*'s decision is final and binding if neither Party has notified the other within the times required by this contract that he intends to refer the matter to the *tribunal*.

Review by the *tribunal* 93.4   A Party may refer a dispute to the *tribunal* if

- the Party is dissatisfied with the *Adjudicator*'s decision or
- the *Adjudicator* did not notify a decision within the time allowed and a new adjudicator has not been chosen,

except that neither Party may refer a dispute to the *tribunal* unless they have notified the other Party of their intention to do so not more than four weeks after the end of the time allowed for the *Adjudicator*'s decision.

contract forms

conditions of contract

▰nec®3 Supply Short Contract

Contract Forms are indexed by Page number with a prefix p. Conditions of Contract (CC) are indexed by clause numbers (main clause heads by **bold numbers**). Terms in *italics* are identified in Contract Data, and defined terms have capital initial letters.
